Poems for our Planet

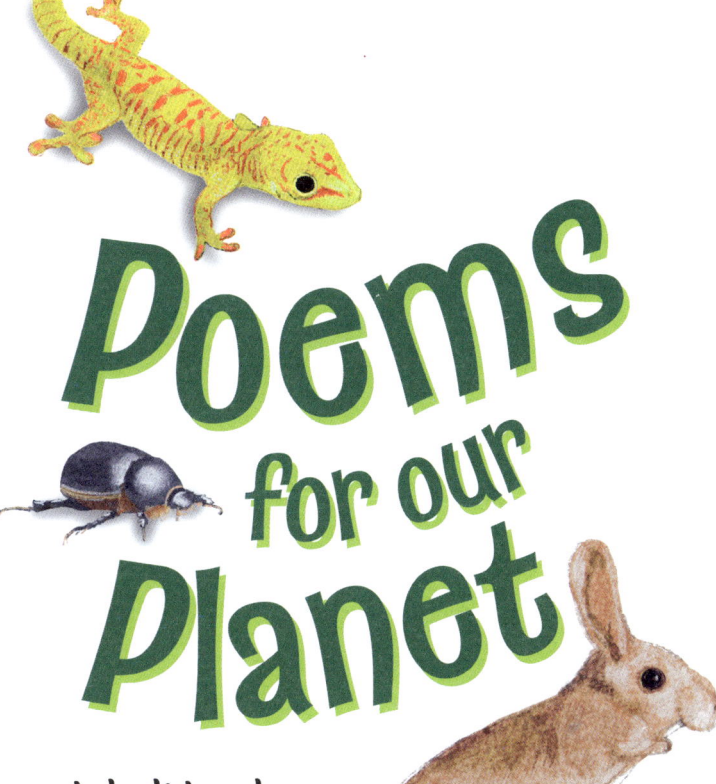

Poems for our Planet

Inbali Iserles

Illustrated by
Doris Shermadhi,
Alex Aldrich Barrett and
Sally Garland

Collins

Contents

- BONUS Biomes 6
- BONUS Biomes map 8
- Chapter 1 A Journey into the Tundra 11
- BONUS Krill 24
- Chapter 2 A Journey into Grasslands 27
- BONUS Colour communication 40
- Chapter 3 A Journey into Freshwater 43
- BONUS Whirligig beetles 56
- Chapter 4 A Journey into Saltwater 59
- BONUS Zones of the ocean 72
- Chapter 5 A Journey into the Desert 75
- Chapter 6 A Journey into the Forest 89
- BONUS Biomes from space 102
- Glossary 104
- About the illustrator 105
- About the author 108
- Book chat 110

Biomes

Biomes are areas of the planet that have similar climates, habitats, plant life and animals.

Tundra

Grassland

Forest

Freshwater

Saltwater

Desert

BONUS

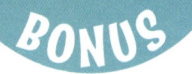

Biomes map

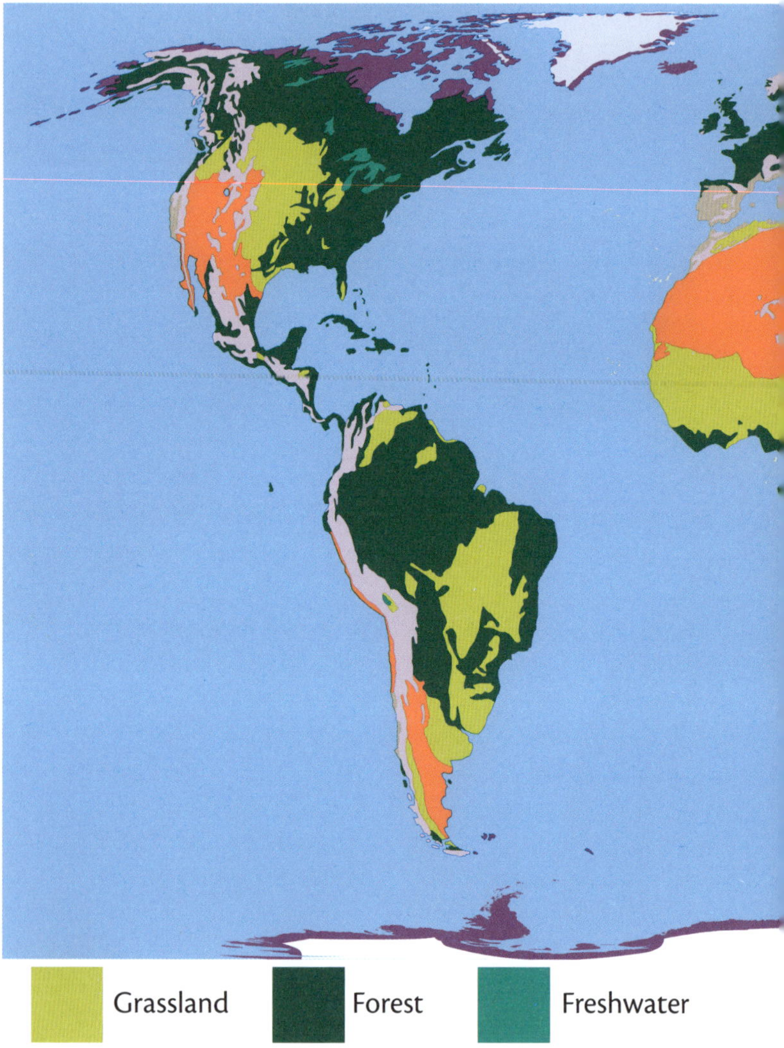

Grassland
Forest
Freshwater

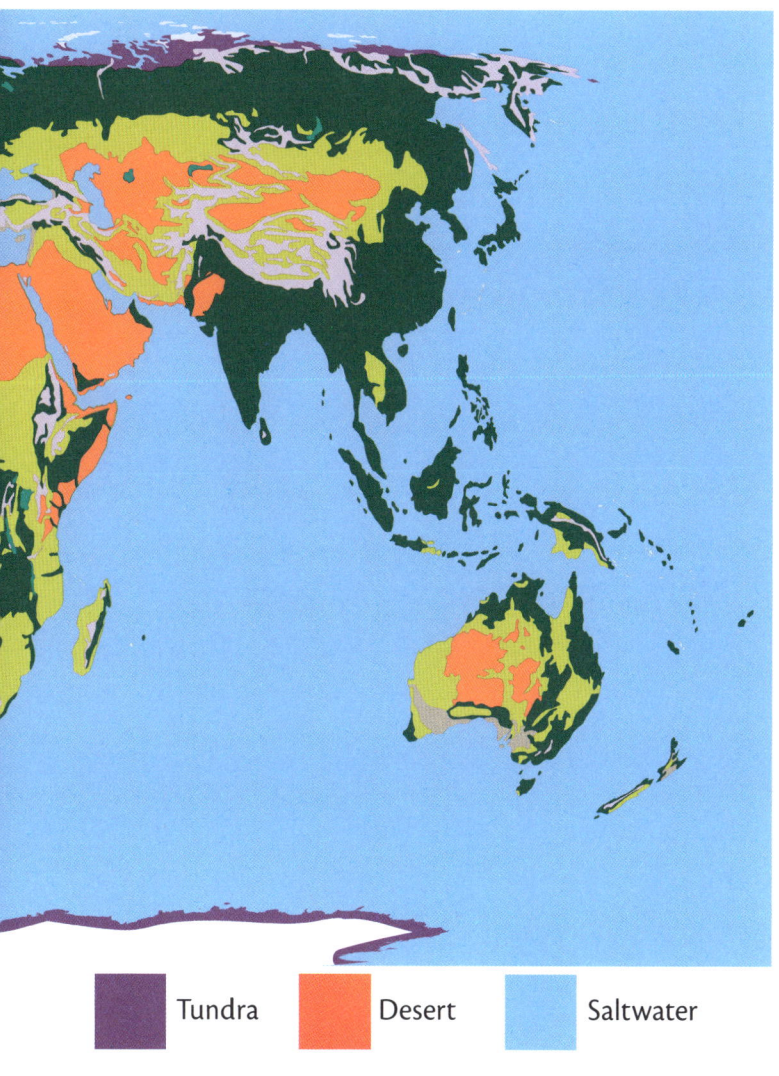

Chapter 1

A Journey into the Tundra

Step into the world of wild winds and wintry chills. The tundra covers large parts of the Arctic. There is also tundra in the far south of the planet across areas of Antarctica.

A world without trees

Some of the tundra is mountainous, with high, jagged peaks. Other areas are flat. But all regions of this biome have one thing in common: there are no trees in the tundra. The ground here is too cold for their roots. It is often covered in deep layers of ice called 'permafrost'. Instead of trees, low shrubs and mosses grow. These plants provide food for animals that live here, like Arctic caribou, also called reindeer. The caribou have fuzzy coats, and wide feet that help them walk on snow and ice. They cover large areas of the tundra, moving in giant herds of 100,000 caribou – or more!

Long, dark winters

Because no trees grow in the tundra, it is hard to find shelter. Winters are long, dark and bitterly cold. Ice and snow paint the land white. The creatures that live here are uniquely adapted to survive the difficult climate.

Adaptation is a process by which animals, plants and fungi develop features that help them to survive. For example, cats have excellent night vision, which allows them to hunt in the moonlight, while ducks have webbed feet, meaning that they can paddle on rivers and lakes. Arctic polar bears have thick undercoats and oily outer fur. This stops seawater reaching their skin.

When food is scarce, polar bears can enter a deep sleep for weeks, or even months. This helps them survive harsh winters in the tundra.

Polar bear

Midwinter tundra
polar bear in velvet sleep
dreams of endless night

Visitors to the tundra

Some animals that live in the tundra are just passing through, like **migrating** eider ducks. They nest on rocky islands in the far north, keeping safe from predators such as Arctic foxes and Arctic wolves. Their plumage of thick feathers is famous for being incredibly warm. They use the feathers to line their nests, protecting their chicks from the icy winds. Eider ducks lose their plumage in a process called 'moulting'. They are unable to fly until their new feathers grow.

Eider Duck is Out of Luck

There once was a stout eider duck
who never did have that much luck.
In warm summer weathers
her hot winter feathers
stayed put, leaving too much to pluck.

The stout eider duck used her beak
to pull out the feathers and seek
a plumage more light,
but she couldn't take flight
as she'd plucked out too much with her beak.

The poor eider duck was irate.
The rest of her flock wouldn't wait!
But her plumage soon grew
and, thank goodness, she flew
in good time for the winter migrate.

Residents of the tundra

Polar bears, Arctic foxes and Arctic hares do not migrate. They spend their whole lives in the northern tundra. Similarly, Adélie and emperor penguins live in Antarctica's tundra all their lives.

Adélie Penguins

Across the sea ice
we waddle, slither and slide
like clowns: but look twice!
We are masters of water.
Under the waves, watch us glide!

Eat or be eaten

Every year, huge numbers of Adélie penguins shuffle over the sea ice as wind batters their feathers. They survive on krill (tiny shrimp) that cluster under the ice. As the penguins hunt the krill, they must be watchful: giant leopard seals stalk the freezing waters of Antarctica, seeking out tasty meals like passing penguins.

The colours of summer

During spring and summer, large patches of pink and orange heathers burst into flower. Yellow gorse and white cotton grass blossom sweeps over the land. But even in summer, it is never hot in the tundra, and racing winds bring in sleet and storms.

The struggle for survival

Arctic foxes climb the cliffs of the northern tundra where sea birds nest in huge numbers. The foxes hunt chicks that have just fledged – young birds that are only just learning to fly. The chicks are easier prey than adults. But the adult birds try to protect their chicks, just as the adult foxes attempt to feed their cubs. Every day in the tundra is a battle for survival.

The Mountain

Seasons change on the mountain.
A cold wind rises,
silver grass
stands stiff in the hiss
of an Arctic breeze.
Clouds roll in on the mountain,
gusts and gales
of thick white mist
that bring whirls, and winds, and flurries.
Down comes the rain
on the rocks and the ridges,
running and roiling,
slipping and seething.
It streams down the mountain's shoulders.
But the mountain is strong:
it has held its ground over millions of years,
seen winds rise and rest;
ice thicken and thaw.
The mountain does not crumble.

Birds flutter in flocks on the mountain,
squawking, clacking, bustling, flapping;
feathers in flurries like snow on the peaks.
They bring furtive foxes,
a fire-eyed falcon.
Battles break out on the mountain:
the clashing of caribou,
clatter of antlers;
drama and danger,
the drumming of hooves
kick up dark-dancing dust like a fog.
The dust freckles and speckles the mountain's face.
But the mountain is sturdy:
it was forged by flame
from the fires of Earth.
It burst from the sea into lava
and boulders
and grit.
The mountain does not crumble.

The mountain endures:
the howling nights of winter's hail,
when the sun slinks low,
below the horizon.
The mountain endures:
the fiery flashes of summer sun,
and winter's shivering showers.
It is white in summer with cottongrass flowers;
it is white in winter with a cape of snow.
As the story of life and death plays out on its peaks.
As fox cubs gambol and grow and go on to hunt
the chicks that flourish and fledge and fly and flee.
Seasons change on the mountain
but the mountain does not change.
For the mountain is strong.
The mountain is sturdy.
The mountain does not crumble.

Krill

Krill can be found in oceans all around the world – there are over 85 different species of these little shrimp-like creatures! Most of them are only 1 to 2 centimetres long, but they're of huge importance as food for larger creatures like penguins, dolphins and even the massive blue whale.

a swarm of krill

Did you know that a single blue whale can eat up to four tons of krill in a single day? Perhaps it's just as well that krill can lay vast numbers of eggs – an adult krill can lay up to 10,000 eggs at one time!

a whale eating krill

Chapter 2

A Journey into Grasslands

The sun beats down on the grasslands. This biome covers large open areas full of different kinds of grasses. Unlike the tundra, trees grow here, but they are spaced out. This is because grasslands tend to be dry, without enough rainfall for lots of trees.

Places to hide

Forests provide plenty of places to hide, but most grasslands don't. Standing out can be dangerous if you are prey and someone wants to eat you – and if you're the predator, it might stop you getting your lunch! Grassland animals have developed clever ways to blend in. For example, spotted hyenas live in the African savannah, a type of grassland. Their creamy brown coats are dappled with black spots, merging with the colours of the grasses and shrubs.

Spotted hyenas are often portrayed as villains. People call them **scavengers**, or say they are ugly. In fact, hyenas are excellent hunters. They live in large clans ruled by a female leader, and are caring parents to their cubs. And as for beauty? Surely it's in the eye of the beholder!

Hyena

I am a hyena
Do you see me for what I am?
A creature of the African savannah
Wild and untamed
Without admiration and respect
How can you bear to look at me?
No more than a scavenger
A bully and a thief
A heartless beast without family
    or tribe
I am not
Elegant and beautiful
A member of a clan
An animal that is loyal and true
A caring parent to my cubs
Do you see me for what I am?
I am a hyena

Now read it again from the bottom!

Speaking in colour

While some animals use camouflage to hide, others stand out. Chameleons do both! Chameleons are a group of lizards that live in grasslands, forests and desert biomes around the world. They have an incredible skill: they can change the colour of their scales. They do this to hide from predators, to attract mates and to adjust their temperatures. They even change colours to share their feelings!

The Colour King

I have a lot of feelings.
I wear them as colours:
a dazzling rainbow when I am scared.
A silvery dance of greys and red.
I live to impress:
do you prefer me yellow?
Or purple and pink?
I'm cleverer than you think:
I am the colour king.
I use the rainbow to show you how I feel.
My emotions are real:
anger,
fear,
and above all, love.
Look at my beauty: could you fail to love me back?
Let me glimmer,
and shimmer,
and change for you.
My dear: whatever you ask,
I'm up for the task.
Let me be your kaleidoscope!

An ever-evolving hue, but not just for you.
To keep me warm, or cool.
Navy blue like the night in the blistering heat of the sun.
Pale like milk when the air grows cold.
I am bold.
Imposters see me and quake with fear!
My rainbow flecks are brighter than theirs.
Orange like fire,
the crimson lick of flame.
I do not blame them when they run.
If I saw myself, I would run too.
I am changing; always changing.
I speak with the rainbow.
I don't need words to tell you I am near:
I am bold,
I am fearless,
I am here.

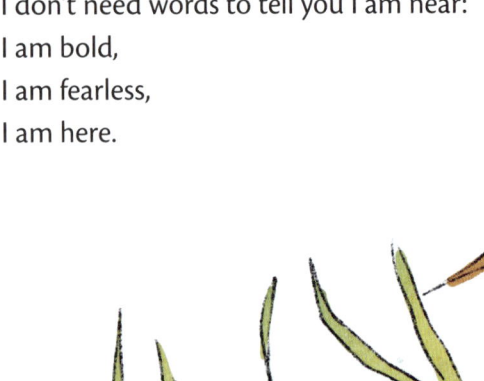

Cute but not always cuddly

Grasslands around the world are home to a wide variety of animals, from the lizards and kangaroos of the Australian Outback to African lions, bush elephants and meerkats.

Meerkats may look cute, but they are ferocious when under attack! They live in large groups called 'mobs', led by a **dominant** male and female. Members of the mob take it in turn to act as lookouts. They guard the mob's burrow, rearing on their hind legs to spy for predators like the poisonous puff adder. And while meerkats mostly eat insects, they will happily feast on a snake if they catch one!

Spy Watch Meerkat Saves the Day

Brown eyes
Small size
Quick-thinker
Fruit-drinker
Looks sweet
Loves meat
Seems charming
Snake harming
Spy watch:
Top notch!
Pricked ears
Spy hears
Strange creak
Squeak! Squeak!
Friends arrive
Snake! Alive!
Puff adder
Cub-grabber
Striped stranger
Great danger!

Spy race
Snake chase
Snake sought:
Snake caught
Snake slay
Saves day
Spy proud
Feeds crowd
Shares treat
Cubs eat
Gang amazed
Spy praised!
Snake-nobbler
Scale-gobbler
Snake-cruncher
Scale-muncher
Snake-trapper
Tooth-snapper
Belly-filler
Snake-killer!

Changing habitats

Like all habitats, grasslands have been affected by climate change. Some animals are particularly **vulnerable** to changes in their environments, and this was true of a little rodent called the Bramble Cay melomys. Bramble Cay is a tiny island off the coast of Papua New Guinea. When climate change led to rising floods, the melomys could not escape its island home. Its habitat was destroyed, and the melomys vanished. Tragically, the Bramble Cay melomys was the first recorded mammal to become extinct because of climate change.

In Memory of the Bramble Cay Melomys

Declared extinct because of climate change, May 2015

It lived upon an island in the sea,
a tiny piece of land called Bramble Cay.
The waters rose: the rodent could not flee.
The little melomys was washed away.

In memory of its soft brown fur, its tail,
its nose, its whiskers and its shining eyes,
let passing ships drop flags and lower sails,
to mourn the melomys with sad goodbyes.

Farewell small island rodent, gone too soon,
lost to the waves as waters rose and swirled.
We dip our heads under a scarlet moon,
and weep for your extinction from our world.

Colour communication

Chameleons change colour in a truly amazing way. They do it by altering the position of tiny crystals in their skin. This affects how the crystals reflect light — which makes the chameleons appear to change colour!

This bright green Parson's chameleon blends in perfectly with the leaves in the Madagascan jungle where it lives.

This is also a Parson's chameleon! It can change colour to match the lichen and bark on this branch.

Chapter 3

A Journey into Freshwater

Step inside a watery wonderland of lakes, rivers and streams. Freshwater biomes are found all over the world. Here we can discover fish such as carp and pike. **Amphibians** like frogs and newts bob on the surface of the water or watch from the bank. Birds like herons and curlews wade through the shallows, while mammals like otters frisk and play, chasing through grasses and diving down into the silty water.

The Otter

A shiver of light on the morning lake.
Wake! And slip down the bank unseen.
The otter's body as quick as a fish.
Swish! The gentle flick of her tail.
Billows of water that ripple and rush.
Hush as the otter dives below:
The magic place where the river fish go.

In the murky water, the scent of earth.
Her body as slim as a stalking cat.
Her whiskery cat-face searches her lair
With a cool and attentive hunter's eye;
With care through the quiet of bobbing reeds.
She feeds and rests as the sun climbs high,
And naps on the bank under bright blue sky.

Danger in the deep

Snakes are scaly reptiles that exist in a wide range of biomes. In rainforests, they climb trees or stalk the forest floor. In deserts, they slip across the sand. But the largest snakes on Earth – green anacondas – are found in freshwater biomes. They lurk, unseen, in the gloom. Green anacondas live in the rivers of South American rainforests. The females are much larger than the males, reaching almost 9 metres when fully grown – that's the length of five or six adult humans joined together! They eat fish, frogs, deer and even caimans, which are cousins of alligators. Would you dare to enter their waters?

Anaconda

Amazon giant: as long as a bus
Nighttime hunter sniffs the air
Angled head and button eyes
Camouflaged in the silty depths
Or lurks unseen in dappled grass
Nudges reeds with angled head
Darkness is her stalking time
Amazon giant: her real name is dread

The world of insects

Freshwater habitats attract thousands of different kinds of minibeast. They include stinging or biting insects like midges and bees, other flying insects like dragonflies and butterflies, and swimmers like whirligig beetles.

Born underwater

Many insects start life underwater. For example, dragonflies, damselflies and mayflies all hatch in ponds, rivers and streams and spend the first part of their lives under the surface. It is only when they become adults that these insects grow wings and take to the skies.

Helping our waterways

Whirligig beetles have short, paddle-like back legs. They use them to swim over the surface of lakes and ponds while their slender front legs grab flies that fall into the water. Young whirligig beetles – known as beetle larvae – live under the surface of the water, where they feed on tiny insects. By eating the little creatures that fall into the lake, the whirligig beetles help to keep the water clear and clean. It is easy to overlook tiny animals like whirligig beetles but they are vital to the health of our waterways, and of our planet.

Whirligig Jig

Whirligig, water jig,
glide on the pond with a zag and zig.
Paddling feet, hunt to eat,
circle the water in search of treat.
Here comes crow: dive below!
Hurry small whirligig: go, go, go!
Sun shines bright, crow takes flight,
whirligig beetle is back in sight.

Whirligig, water jig,
glide on the pond with a zag and zig.
Spring on prey, feed by day,
any small creature that's in its way.
In a flash: fly goes splash!
Whirligig jaws go gnash, gnash, gnash!
Flies are best! Beetle at rest,
riding the water's silvery crest.

Whirligig, water jig,
Glide on the pond with a zag and zig.
Waters flow, sun sinks low.
Sunset shimmers in colourful glow.
Day to night: bats take flight!
Soar over water in fading light.
Foxes creep; one last sweep
as whirligig beetle drifts to sleep.

One Million Voices

One million voices of insects that sway:
a blizzard of bodies around a lake.
The midges that clot in a thick grey cloud
and bees that buzz at the end of the day.

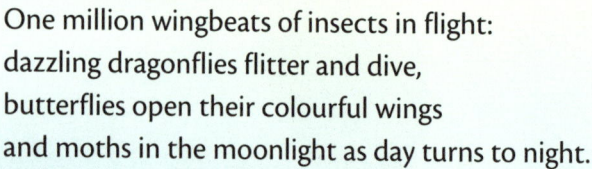

One million bodies of insects unseen:
the scurrying ants in the long damp grass,
the tiny green larvae that cling to leaves
are camouflaged within layers of green.

One million wingbeats of insects in flight:
dazzling dragonflies flitter and dive,
butterflies open their colourful wings
and moths in the moonlight as day turns to night.

One million insects that glide on a lake:
whirligig beetles with paddling back legs,
swimming and circling the clear blue water.
Skating the surface and making it quake.

One million heartbeats yet only a sigh
of hatchlings that climb out of tiny eggs.
They feed frogs and birds; help the flowers thrive:
the invisible fabric of earth and sky.

Changing views of nature

Hundreds of years ago, most people had different ideas about wildlife than they do today. They thought that plants were there to look pretty, or to provide food – plants that didn't fit these ideas were called 'weeds'. Many animals were hunted for their skins, or because they were 'pests'. In the UK, beavers suffered this fate.

Beavers are mammals that build **dams** out of driftwood. They live on the dams, which keeps them safe from most predators – but it did not keep them safe from humans. People thought of beavers as a nuisance because their dams slowed down the free flow of water, and hunters trapped them for their fur. As a result, by about 500 years ago, there were no beavers left in Britain. But beavers are returning to UK rivers. We now know that their dam-building helps prevent floods by slowing down the flow of rivers. The calmer waters around their dams create habitats for different types of insects, birds and fish.

In a complex habitat, don't all creatures have a role?

Whirligig beetles

Whirligig beetles are small, oval-shaped beetles that whirl around on the surface of ponds. Their back legs are shaped like paddles, which helps them skim along on the water.

whirligig beetles close up

a swarm of whirligig beetles

Chapter 4

A Journey into Saltwater

Dive into the largest biome on Earth. Three quarters of our world is covered in saltwater. Here we find a range of habitats like coral reefs packed with colourful fish, and underwater kelp forests where sea otters live. An enormous variety of life thrives in our oceans, including fish, sea turtles, dolphins and seals.

Marine mammals

Mammals are warm-blooded animals that give birth to live babies and feed them on milk. A huge number of mammals are furry land animals, like cats, monkeys, foxes and bears. But the ocean is home to many species of marine mammals. These include manatees that float in underwater kelp forests, walruses that bask upon beaches and small whales called narwhals that are famous for their unicorn-like horns.

Life in a pod

Dolphins are playful, intelligent marine mammals. They eat fish and krill, which are tiny shrimp-like creatures that live in the sea. Dolphins live in extended families called pods. New Zealand's dusky dolphins typically live in pods of up to 15 members. These pods come together at certain times of year to form bigger groups of hundreds or even thousands of dolphins.

The Ballad of the Dusky Dolphin

There was a dusky dolphin calf
who played upon the seas.
She frolicked with her pod and lived
a life of peace and ease.

Until a storm rolled on the sea
with waves as black as night,
that drove her spinning through the deep
and gave her such a fright.

And when the dolphin rose for air
the waves finally banished,
she called her pod to come to her
to find her pod had vanished.

She swam the frozen waters of
Antarctica through ice;
She saw a group of friendly seals
and stopped to get advice.

"Not here!" said they, "Go north my friend
to where the orcas sail.
Go forth and find the narwhal with
a diamond on his tail."

And so the dolphin swam long leagues
along the orcas' way,
and found the narwhal with the tail
who solemnly did say:

"Not here, my friend, you must be brave:
the walruses live west.
Go seek the walrus with black eyes,
his knowledge is the best."

The lonely dolphin swam out west
where seas were fierce and blue,
and found the walrus with black eyes
and said, "How do you do?"

The walrus viewed her with disdain.
He said, "Dolphin, begone!
I warned your pod, I'm warning you:
I won't stay patient long."

"You saw my pod?" the dolphin cried.
"They passed this rocky shore?"
"I did indeed," the walrus said.
"One hundred – maybe more!"

The dolphin heard their pips and cries,
her people's song! The thrill!
It struck her like a bolt of light:
they're following the krill!

The dusky dolphins sprang for joy,
their play wild and excited.
And with them she'll forever stay,
now that they're reunited.

A dusky dolphin's happiest
when she is free to roam.
As long as she is with her pod,
she's never far from home.

Sea birds

Birds like albatrosses nest on mountains overlooking the water. When it's time to choose a mate, the male sits on a nest and invites a female to land. Once she does, he clicks, calls and dances. If she starts to dance too, they are likely to become mates! Albatross couples usually stay together their whole lives.

The Dance of the Albatross

The albatross is keen to find his mate,
And he will do whatever must be done;
With other males he can't sit back and wait,
He will not quit until her heart is won:
He bows his head and starts to dip and dance,
He sings to her: a clack, a screech, a cluck,
His great wings raised to put her in a trance;
He hopes, with this, that he will be in luck,
But sadly others also squawk and sing,
And try to show the female they're the best.
With spins and noise and battering of wing,
They put his heartfelt efforts to the test.
    Yet thankfully the female dances too!
    And so the male knows that her love is true.

Chasing the sun

Most species of albatross migrate long distances. But the birds with the longest migration are Arctic terns. Every year, the terns travel all the way from the Arctic Circle in the far north of the Earth to Antarctica in the far south. The terns do this to escape the wild winters at both poles. They chase the sun 35,000 kilometres!

Arctic tern

Longest migration
birds flee winter for the sun
memories of home

The deep

Some of the most extraordinary creatures on Earth are found in our oceans. Even their names sound fantastical: for example, how would you like to meet a giant sea spider, a dumbo octopus, a vampire squid or a black seadevil anglerfish?

One of the most famous residents of the deep sea is the blobfish. Blobfish live in the midnight zone, where sunlight does not reach. On land, people call them ugly or grumpy-looking, because of their droopy faces. But these fish look different in their natural environment. The **water pressure** in the midnight zone is very strong – it would crush normal animal bones! Blobfishes' squishy bodies help them survive.

Ode to a Blobfish

I am a fish
most rarely seen,
and then just on the telly.
When I am caught
the people say
I look like wobbly jelly.
My gloomy face
and blobby nose
aren't for the world above me.
With wide-lipped frown
I'm always told
only my mum could love me.
I'm from the deep
and down below
my squishy face looks fresher.

My boneless shape
works well down here
to counteract the pressure.
The other fish
down in the deep
insist I'm quite the catch.
When others try
to rival me
they learn they've met their match.
Swim down deeper
if you should dare,
you'll see that I'm a cutie.
A real keeper,
bizarre and rare,
the ocean's natural beauty!

BONUS
Zones of the ocean

sunlight

twilight

midnight

lower midnight

hadal

Chapter 5

A Journey into the Desert

Welcome to the heat of the desert. This is the driest biome on Earth. While rainforests receive over 2,000 millimetres of rainfall a year, deserts get less than 300 millimetres. It can be very hot in the daytime, but once the sun goes down, the temperature can drop by 40 degrees Celsius. That's like stepping straight from a hot summer's day into a freezer.

Under the scorching sun

It's tough to survive in the desert. A lack of water means most trees can't grow here. Instead, there are cacti – plants that are suited to the conditions. One of the largest cacti on Earth is the saguaro (pronounced 'sa-wah-roe'). It lives in the Sonora Desert between the Southeast US and Central America. A saguaro can grow 12 metres high. That's roughly the height of a three-storey building!

Saguaros grow slowly and live for around 200 years. They can survive months without rainfall. Their network of roots draws water from deep under the sand, which they store in their fleshy bodies. Standing tall in the desert, saguaros look like great, green statues or even sentinels – silent guards that watch over the burning land.

Saguaro

I am a keeper of secrets,
a watchful eye of the desert.
For two hundred years
I've looked out
on this land.

The silent sentinel of the sand.
My thick green arms
embrace the air.
My roots explore the
    rocky ground.

I watch
but make no sound.
I'm still and calm,
keep nervous lizards
safe from harm.

My blooms give food
to bird and bee.
Do not question me:
I will not speak the secrets
that I see.

Ancient life

You might think that it would be hard for any animal to survive in a place as dry as a desert. Yet some of the Earth's most ancient creatures live here, such as scorpions. Scorpions existed before the age of the dinosaurs. They have eight hairy legs and a hard skeleton on the outside of their bodies. Scorpions are incredibly tough. They are cold-blooded, meaning that their body temperature changes with their environment. They can survive intense heat and freezing cold. They can go months without food. And they have a special weapon: a poisonous stinger in their tails.

A Sting in the Tail

Oh clumsy-footed human, please beware!
I may be shy but I am not a fool.
Tread lightly as you walk across my land:
watch out for tell-tail patterns in the sand.

I prowl this desert on eight hairy legs.
I hunt for little lizards, snakes and bugs.
I do not seek your kind, that much is true,
but step on me and I will step on you.

I'll click my crab-like pincers at your feet
and hiss to scare you, hoping you will go.
And if you do not quickly change your trail,
you'll find I have a stinger in my tail.

Away now, human, I won't tell you twice!
Go seek the lazy comforts of the shade.
The desert world is mine to hunt and roam,
and you are safer staying in your home.

I hope you've heard me and you've understood
that it is wise to keep away from me.
If you ignore this warning, you will fail,
and I'll be forced to kiss you with my tail.

Warm-blooded animals

While many desert-dwellers are cold-blooded, some warm-blooded animals are found in this biome, like camels, coyotes and fennec foxes. These animals must keep a constant body temperature even when it is very hot or cold outside. One warm-blooded desert animal is a rodent called a jerboa.

Desert rodents

Jerboas live in the deserts of Asia and North Africa. With rabbit ears and kangaroo legs, they look like someone has pieced together bits of different animals! But jerboas are suited to survive the harsh climate. They burrow underground in the heat of the day. When out on the sand, their huge ears are perfect for listening for predators like snakes and foxes. Perhaps most incredible of all, jerboas do not run – they jump! If scared, a tiny jerboa can leap 3 metres in a single bound. That's the height of a basketball hoop!

Jumping Jerboa

Jumping jerboa.
Every part borrowed from a different beast:
Rabbit ears, a mouse's body. Kangaroo legs like springs.
Bounce! Bounce!
Others are left in her dust.
Across the desert sand: bounce! Bounce!

Desert insects

Like almost everywhere on Earth, insects are found in the desert. Ants build large underground nests to protect themselves from the blistering sun. Nighttime moths flutter between cactus blossoms, sipping their nectar and pollinating the flowers so that their seeds can grow.

'Scarab' dung beetles

Scarab beetles, also known as dung beetles, survive the heat of North Africa's Sahara Desert. They gather animal poo, which they roll into balls. The beetles shunt the balls along the sand into the shade, where they feast upon them. Yes, that's right: the beetles eat poo! The poo is cooler than the sand, and it provides shade to the beetles while they munch. In eating the poo, the beetles help to recycle other animals' waste. They also reduce the number of flies in the desert, as there's less poo for flies to feed on.

The ancient Egyptians worshipped dung beetles. They believed that the way the beetles rolled balls of dung symbolised the sun moving through the sky. The Ancient Egyptians carved statues of dung beetles and wore dung beetle 'scarab' jewellery for good luck.

Dung Beetle

Since the time of the dinosaurs,
many ages of the moon,
I've rolled dung, or guano (you call it poo).
It's nothing new:
the very essence of life itself.
I am the sacred scarab, collector and recycler of waste.
To goats it is simply their droppings,
left to steam in the heat of the day,
left to decay.
Discovered on the sand like precious gold.
Or the jewelled crowns of the ancient pharaohs.
I gather my treasure
(I roll my lunch)
like the sun that rolls over the sky.

Chapter 6

A Journey into the Forest

Step into the world of trees, where birdsong fills the air. The first living things you might notice in a forest are the trees – but they're not the only ones! Forests are home to all kinds of life, from the tiniest lichens (which are part fungi, part plant) to great apes like chimpanzees. There are three main habitats within the forest biome: snow forests, rainforests and **temperate** forests.

Snow forests

Snow forests grow to the south of the northern tundra. Many of the trees are evergreens, like pines and spruce – they do not shed their leaves. Animals like bobcats, wolves and owls live in snow forests. Their thick fur or feathers keep them warm as winter temperatures plunge well below zero.

Wolf Hunt

She stands in the quiet of falling snow
ears rotating: forward, back.
She waits till she knows which way to go:
a hoof,
a snort,
a twig goes *crack*!

She slips unseen between the trees,
even her puffy tail won't sway.
She leads the pack with skilful ease:
one ear
goes flick,
This way!

They cross the forest through the night.
They stalk the unsuspecting deer.
The wolves close in as it grows light:
three front;
six to
the rear.

The deer is spooked; the wolves give chase,
eyes on their leader; eyes on their prey.
It is the wolves that win the race.
Their cubs
will feed
today.

Rainforests

Rainforests are hot and wet all year round. Millions of animals, plants and fungi thrive here. Birds like toucans and macaws, mammals like howler monkeys and giant anteaters, and countless snakes, frogs and insects live in rainforests. You also find plants like stinky titan arums!

Titan arums

Titan arums are huge, rare plants that grow in the Indonesian rainforest. Their flowers cling to a central spear. Most blooms attract butterflies and birds with their sweet smells. Titan arums are different: their flowers attract flies with their pong of rotting meat!

Titan Arum

There is a plant,
it has a bloom
that smells of rotting meat.
It grows in dark
and leafy gloom
within the forest heat.
The other flowers
in the jungle
lure birds in great flocks.
But titan's spear is wicked
and it smells worse than your socks!
The birds think 'yuck!'
on sniffing titan:
quickly they take flight.
The bats think 'gross!'
A stench to frighten
(as it's worse at night).
Most animals agree with them.
Of titan, they aren't trusting.
Because the pong is gag-worthy
and frankly quite disgusting!

Temperate forests

Temperate forests have milder climates than snow forests and more varied temperatures than rainforests. Here you experience all four seasons: autumn, winter, spring and summer. Trees are usually deciduous: they lose leaves in autumn and sprout new ones in spring.

Mysterious-looking fungi grow in here with names like waxcap, stinkhorn, and even turkey tail! The mushrooms – the fruiting part of the fungi – are the bits that poke out of the soil like the tip of an iceberg. The rest of these living things grow far beneath forests and heath. Fungi might look like plants, but they are different – and much more ancient.

Fungus

In forest green
unheard; unseen,
it pokes its way through sprigs of grass,
through twisted twigs,
grows at a slant
between the shoots
and fallen leaves.
It's not a plant.

From world beneath,
and without teeth,
it munches old and rotting wood,
through splitting bark,
grows at a slant,
in bulb-like shapes,
or under roots,
but it's no plant.

It needs no light;
it likes the night,
makes shapes that thrill,
makes shapes that fright.
It has no leaves;
it thrives in dark,
while others can't:
for it's no plant.

One world

Each biome creates habitats for different kinds of wildlife, and each habitat plays an essential role in the survival of our planet. We live in a world of diversity and wonder: from the great polar bears of the tundra to the grassland hyenas; from the tiny insects that swim around a freshwater lake to the dusky dolphins that swim through saltwater in pods; from the scorpions that prowl over the desert sand to the stinky titan arum in the heart of the rainforest.

The lungs of the Earth

Forests are places of incredible biodiversity, which means that they are full of different animals, plants and fungi. The trees that live in forests produce a lot of the planet's oxygen, the air that we breathe. For this reason, forests are sometimes called the lungs of the Earth.

Every biome plays a role in the health and survival of our world. But perhaps the forest, more than any other biome, has become a symbol of life on our planet.

I am the Forest

I am the forest
and I am the snail.
I am the ocean
and I am the whale.
I am the fireball light of the sun.
I am the hare on a warm summer's run.

I am the earthworm
and I am the fly.
I am the sparrow
and I am the sky.
I am a moth in the fast-fading light.
I am a bat on a midwinter's night.

I am the grizzly
and I am the roe.
I am the river
and I am the crow.
I am a squirrel that darts through the trees.
I am a dew drop and I am a breeze.

I am the robin
and I am the lake.
I am the ice flats
and I am the hake.
I am a silverfish scuttling through soil.
I am a woodlouse that starts to uncoil.

I am the elephant.
I am the mouse.
I am the antelope.
I am the grouse.
I am a lichen that grows on a tree.
I am a beehive and I am a bee.

I am the mountain
and I am the stream.
I am the ocean
and I am the bream.
I am the tidal wave driving the surf.
I am the forest for I am the Earth.

Bonus

Biomes from space

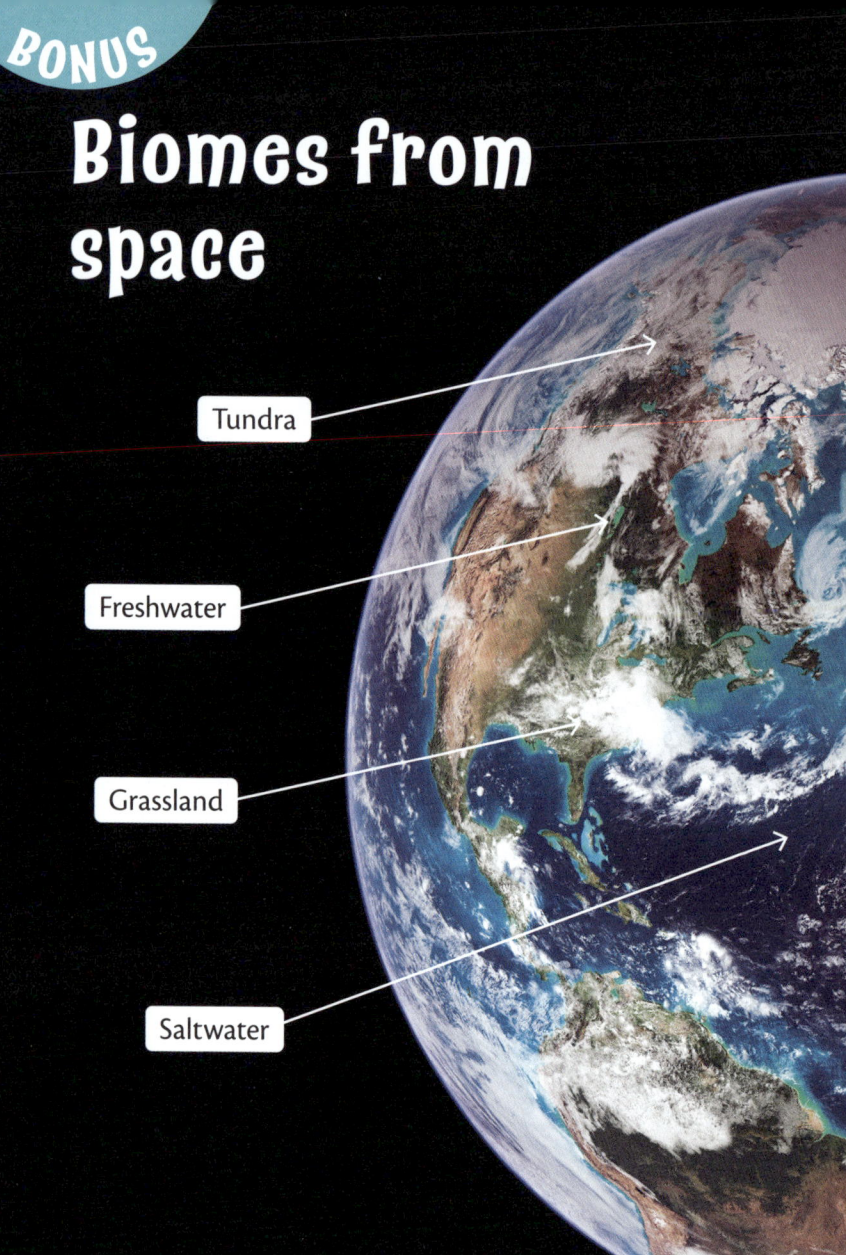

- Tundra
- Freshwater
- Grassland
- Saltwater

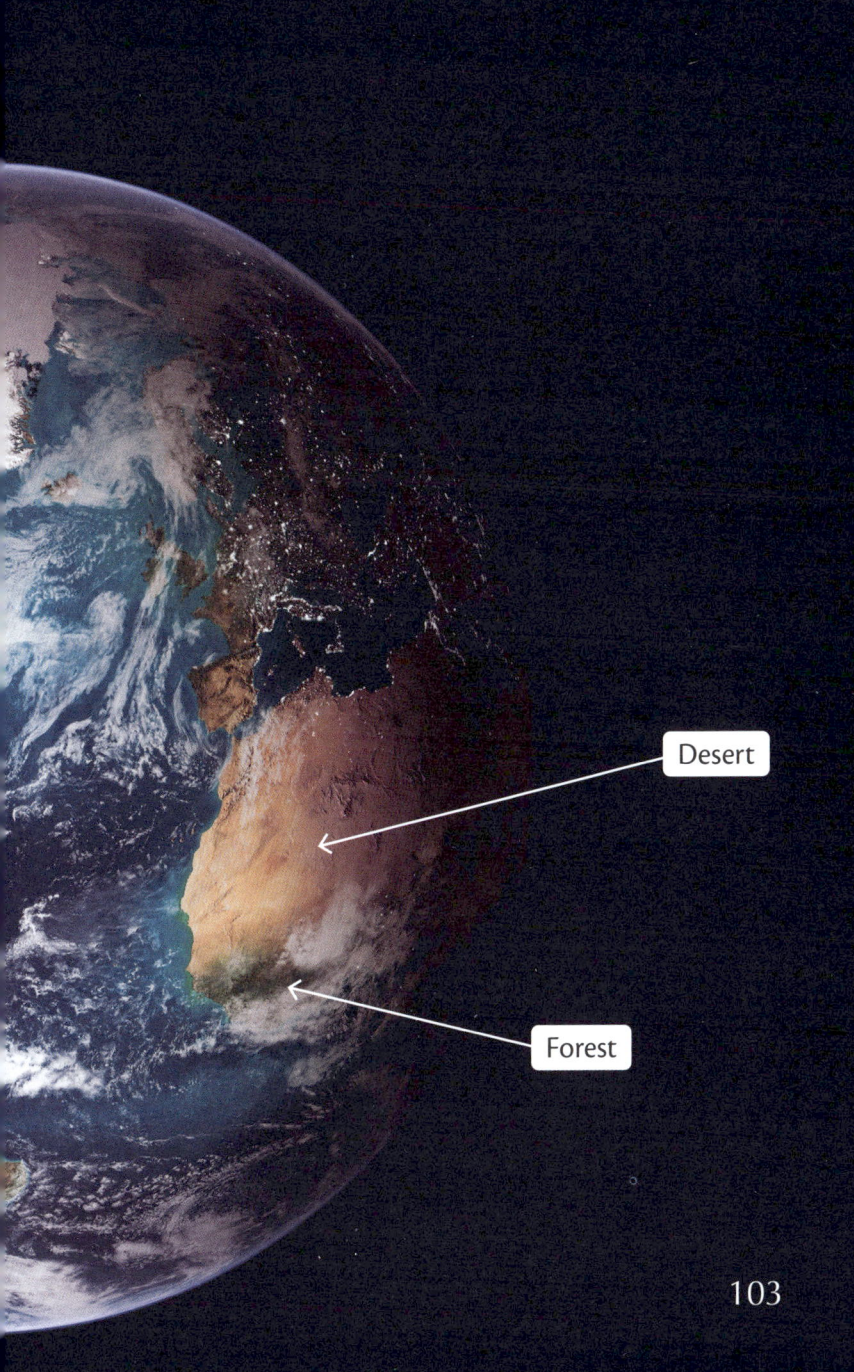

Glossary

amphibians animals that can live in water or on land such as frogs and newts

dams structures that stop or control the flow of a river

dominant in charge or most powerful

migrating moving from one place to another

scavengers animals that feed on dead animals they haven't killed themselves

temperate neither extremely hot nor extremely cold

vulnerable easily hurt or damaged

water pressure the force of water when it pushes against something

About the illustrator

What inspired you to become an illustrator?
The desire to give shape and image to stories, and to everything that lives in my imagination.

Who is your favourite artist?
I deeply admire Isabella Mazzanti, her style is a constant source of inspiration for me.

Doris Shermadhi

What was the first thing you ever illustrated?
My first real illustration came from a school project my sister was working on. She asked me to bring to life a story she had written. I was around 12 or 13 years old. I immediately felt the urge to turn her words into images. That was my first encounter with illustration as a form of storytelling, and perhaps the moment I realised how much I loved bringing stories to life through drawing.

What is your favourite picture in this book?
The polar bear, because it gives me a sense of peace, wonder, and infinity.

Have you visited any of the biomes mentioned?
Yes, I've had the chance to explore forests and grasslands, fascinating environments that left me with a deep sense of connection to nature.

About the illustrator

What inspired you to become an illustrator?
I was always interested in painting and making art, and I think books are really magical. It made sense to be a painter who works on books.

Alex Aldrich Barrett

Who is your favourite artist?
My favourite artist is Trina Schart Hyman, who was a children's book illustrator. She illustrated a lot of very beautiful fairy tales.

What was the first thing you ever illustrated?
The first things I ever illustrated were my own stories that I made up when I was a kid!

What is your favourite picture in this book?
I loved making the drawing of the terns flying.

Have you visited any of the biomes mentioned?
I have spent a lot of time swimming in freshwater streams and lakes and getting to see the amazing wildlife there.

About the illustrator

What inspired you to become an illustrator?
I just loved drawing when I was young, and it seemed like a natural thing for me to do.

Sally Garland

Who is your favourite artist?
I don't really have one favourite artist. I tend to enjoy all sorts of different artists. At the moment, I particularly like Gabrielle Vincent, who wrote and illustrated the Ernest and Celestine books.

What was the first thing you ever illustrated?
Fiddlesticks by Sean Taylor.

What is your favourite picture book?
Where the Wild Things Are by Maurice Sendak.

Have you visited any of the biomes mentioned?
I come from the north of Scotland and was lucky enough to live near a beautiful pine forest.

About the author

What gave you the idea for this book?

I am crazy about wildlife and poetry. I jumped at the opportunity to write a book that draws upon both passions!

What's your favourite thing about writing?

I love being transported into another world, and the careful selection of language that brings that world to life.

Inbali Iserles

How did you go about writing the poems?

I started by considering a good mix of different wildlife for each biome. I was keen to include a diverse range of poetry too! I thought about different types of poem and the secret power of each form. For example, a reverso poem like *Hyena* encourages the reader to think (and read!) twice; a triple limerick, like *Eider Duck is Out of Luck*, is a great opportunity for humour.

Why did you want to combine poetry with non-fiction text?

I thought that non-fiction text about the biomes could provide an interesting context to the poems. Hopefully, these sections help anchor the poems and give a sense of the varied landscapes where our wildlife thrives.

Which of the biomes in the book do you find most intriguing?

I am fascinated by all the biomes, but perhaps the tundra is the most mysterious, as it is only found in the far north and far south of our planet where humans rarely tread. My favourite biomes are forests because they are absolutely packed with life!

Do you have a favourite animal or plant in the book?

I have a soft spot for hyenas. These beautiful animals are often dismissed as no more than nasty predators because of the way they look.

Did you have to do lots of research?

Yes! I am a wildlife fanatic so I know quite a bit about the natural world, but I was careful to research each biome and look into the behaviour of plants, animals and fungi included in my poems.

Which part of the book was most fun to write?

For me, writing non-fiction is easier than writing poetry – but there is nothing more satisfying than when a poem falls into place! Some poems were particularly fun to write, like *Titan Arum*, the poem about the stinky plant.

What do you hope readers will take away from this book?

I hope readers enjoy stepping into each biome; I hope they love reading the poems out loud! Most of all, I hope the poems inspire a love and care for our natural world.

Book chat

What's the most interesting thing you learnt from reading this book?

Have you read any other books that have poetry as well as non-fiction? How does this book compare?

Why do you think the author chose to use both poetry and non-fiction in the book?

Which is your favourite poem in the book and why?

Which of the biomes would you most like to visit, and why?

If you could ask the author one question, what would you say?

Who would you recommend this book to, and why?

Book challenge:

What's your favourite wild animal? Write a poem of your own about it.

Published by Collins
An imprint of HarperCollins*Publishers*

The News Building
1 London Bridge Street
London
SE1 9GF
UK

Macken House
39/40 Mayor Street Upper
Dublin 1
D01 C9W8
Ireland

Inbali Iserles asserts her moral right to be identified as the author of this work.

Text © Inbali Iserles 2025
Design and illustrations © HarperCollins*Publishers* Limited 2025

Maps © Collins Bartholomew Ltd 2022

10 9 8 7 6 5 4 3 2 1

ISBN 978-0-00-876787-7

All rights reserved. No part of this publication may be reproduced, stored in a retrieval system, or transmitted in any form by any means, electronic, mechanical, photocopying, recording or otherwise, without the prior written permission of the Publisher or a licence permitting restricted copying in the United Kingdom issued by the Copyright Licensing Agency Ltd, 5th Floor, Shackleton House, 4 Battle Bridge Lane, London SE1 2HX.

Without limiting the exclusive rights of any author, contributor or the publisher of this publication, any unauthorised use of this publication to train generative artificial intelligence (AI) technologies is expressly prohibited. HarperCollins also exercise their rights under Article 4(3) of the Digital Single Market Directive 2019/790 and expressly reserve this publication from the text and data mining exception.

British Library Cataloguing-in-Publication Data
A catalogue record for this publication is available from the British Library.

Download the teaching notes and word cards to accompany this book at:
http://littlewandle.org.uk/signupfluency/

Get the latest Collins Big Cat news at
collins.co.uk/collinsbigcat

Author: Inbali Iserles
Illustrators: Doris Shermadhi, Alex Aldrich Barrett (Astound Illustration Agency), Sally Garland (Advocate Art)
Publisher: Laura White
Product manager and commissioning editor: Caroline Green
Series editor: Charlotte Raby
Development editor: Catherine Baker
Project manager: Emily Hooton
Copyeditor: Sally Byford
Proofreader: Catherine Dakin
Cover designer: Sarah Finan
Typesetter: 2Hoots Publishing Services Ltd
Production controller: Katharine Willard

Printed in the UK.

 **MIX**
Paper | Supporting responsible forestry
FSC™ C007454

This book contains FSC™ certified paper and other controlled sources to ensure responsible forest management.

For more information visit: www.harpercollins.co.uk/green

Made with responsibly sourced paper and vegetable ink

Scan to see how we are reducing our environmental impact.

Acknowledgements
The publishers gratefully acknowledge the permission granted to reproduce the copyright material in this book. Every effort has been made to trace copyright holders and to obtain their permission for the use of copyright material. The publishers will gladly receive any information enabling them to rectify any error or omission at the first opportunity.

pp6tl & 10 Shab42/Shutterstock, pp6bl & 26 Mockup Cloud/Shutterstock, pp6br & 88 Vytautas Kielaitis/Shutterstock, pp7tl & 42 Damsea/Shutterstock, pp7tr & 58 Damsea/Shutterstock, pp7br & 74 Bloodberry/Shutterstock, p24 Luis Quinta/Nature Picture Library, p25 Minden Pictures/Alamy, p40 Martin Mecnarowski/Shutterstock, p41 Paul Souders/Getty Images, p43 Jgade/Shutterstock, p51 Photostock-Israel/Science Photo Library, p56 EdwardSnow/Getty Images, p57 Natalia Kuzmina/Shutterstock, pp72–73 Alejo Miranda/Shutterstock, p89 Butterfly Hunter/Shutterstock, pp102–103 Rawpixel.com/Shutterstock.